3 1994 01024 4876

SANTA ANA PUBLIC LIBRARY

D0549116

Dropping In On...
CANADA

Lewis K. Parker

J 971 PAR
Parker, Lewis K.
Canada
31994010244876

51
76

A Geography Series

ROURKE BOOK COMPANY, INC.
VERO BEACH, FLORIDA 32964

©1994 Rourke Book Company, Inc.

All rights reserved. No part of this book may be reproduced or utilized in any form or by any means, electronic or mechanical including photocopying, recording, or by any information storage and retrieval system without permission in writing from the publisher.

A Blackbirch Graphics book.

Printed in the United States of America.

Library of Congress Cataloging-in-Publication Data

Parker, Lewis K.
    Canada / Lewis K. Parker.
        p.   cm. — (Dropping in on)
    Includes bibliographic references and index.
    ISBN 1-55916-002-0
    1. Canada—Description and travel—Juvenile literature. 2. Canada—Geography—Juvenile literature. [1. Canada—Description and travel.] I. Title. II. Series.
F1017.P37   1994
917.1—dc20   93-42778
                                                        CIP
                                                        AC

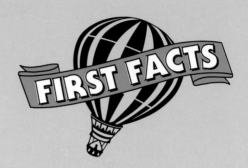

Canada

Official Name: Canada

Area: 3,851,809 square miles

Population: 27,400,000

Capital: Ottawa, Ontario

Largest City: Toronto

Highest Elevation:

Mt. Logan, Yukon Territory

(19, 850 feet)

Official Languages: English, French

Major Religion: Roman Catholic

Money: Canadian dollar

Form of Government:

Constitutional monarchy

TABLE OF CONTENTS

Our Blue Ball—The Earth

The Earth can be divided into two hemispheres. The word hemisphere means "half a ball"—in this case, the ball is the Earth.

The equator is an imaginary line that runs around the middle of the Earth. It separates the Northern Hemisphere from the Southern Hemisphere. North America—where Canada, the United States, and Mexico are located—is in the Northern Hemisphere.

The Northern Hemisphere

When the North Pole is tilted toward the sun, the sun's most powerful rays strike the northern half of the Earth and less sunshine hits the Southern Hemisphere. That is when people in the Northern Hemisphere enjoy summer. When

the North Pole is tilted away from the sun, and the Southern Hemisphere receives the most sunshine, the seasons reverse. Then winter comes to the Northern Hemisphere. Seasons in the Northern Hemisphere and the Southern Hemisphere are always opposite.

ALASKA

BANKS ISLAND

STOP 1

YUKON TERRITORY

• Whitehorse

VICTORIA ISLAND

NORTHWEST TERRITORIES

BRITISH COLUMBIA

ALBERTA

STOP 2

STOP 3

SASKATCHEWAN

MANITOBA

STOP 4

Victoria •

•**Vancouver**

Alberta's Rocky Mountains

The Prairies

Lake Winnipeg

N
W   E
S

UNITED STATES

Lake

Canada

⭐ National Capital

0   miles   500

Get Ready for Canada

Hop into your hot-air balloon. Let's take a trip! You are about to drop in on the largest country in North America. Canada is a huge nation that is divided into provinces and territories.

Canada's geography includes mountains, glaciers, prairies, and lakes.

The northernmost parts of Canada lie within the Arctic Circle. This area is covered by frozen land (tundra) and ice.

Ottawa, Ontario, is the capital of Canada. More than 900,000 people live there.

BAFFIN ISLAND

Hudson Bay

QUEBEC

NEWFOUNDLAND

Labrador Sea

Island of Newfoundland

STOP 6

STOP 7

PRINCE EDWARD ISLAND

NEW BRUNSWICK

ONTARIO

NOVA SCOTIA

Quebec City

STOP 5

Atlantic Ocean

Lake Huron

Ottawa ⭐

Toronto

Lake Ontario

Lake Erie

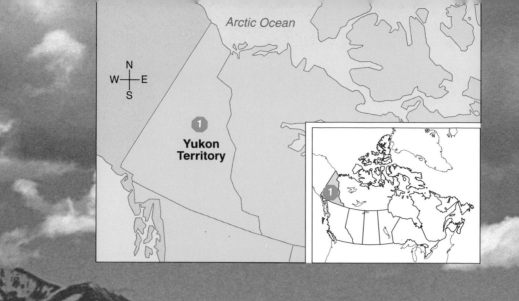

Arctic Ocean

N
W   E
S

Yukon
Territory

Stop 1: Yukon Territory

The first thing you notice about the Yukon Territory is its shape. On a map it looks like a capital "L." The next thing you may notice is its size. It is about 5 times the size of the state of Pennsylvania. The Yukon has rugged mountains and rivers of flowing ice called glaciers.

The largest town in the Yukon is Whitehorse— but only about 21,000 people live here. About

The mountains of Kluane National Park are beautifully reflected in Kathleen Lake.

100 years ago, only 500 people lived in Whitehorse when the gold rush occurred in Canada. Gold was discovered in the Yukon and tens of thousands of people headed here to get rich. Almost overnight, Whitehorse grew from 500 people to more than 20,000!

While we're visiting the Yukon, you can take a boat cruise on the majestic Yukon River. Just outside Whitehorse you can pan for gold.

LET'S TAKE TIME OUT

Many Inuit families live in the northern provinces and territories of Canada. These Inuit children live in the Yukon Territory.

The Inuit: Canada's Native People

The Inuit (Eskimo) are one of the native peoples of Canada. They are scattered in small villages and communities across the coldest parts of Canada. They live in Labrador, in the Northwest Territories, in the Yukon, and along the Arctic Coast.

Many Inuit live much as their ancestors did. They use kayaks (1-person canoes) and umiaks (12-person canoes) to hunt seals and walruses. They also sail out into the ocean in their kayaks and umiaks to spear whales. In the snowy areas where they live, some Inuit use dogsleds to track caribou and polar bears.

Many other Inuit have changed their ways of life. Some have jobs as guides for tourists. Others are miners, truck drivers, teachers, and doctors. They live in modern houses, ride in snowmobiles, send their children to schools, and buy their food in supermarkets.

*Let's travel **south** to Vancouver, in the province of British Columbia. Vancouver is one of Canada's busiest and prettiest port cities.*

The busy harbor of Vancouver is surrounded by the city's tall, modern buildings.

Stop 2: Vancouver

As you come down near Vancouver, British Columbia, you can see tall mountains rising straight out of the Pacific Ocean. You can also smell the scent of cut cedar trees from mills on the Fraser River. You will see forests, and perhaps even a black bear wandering in someone's backyard.

Vancouver is a city that is built right up against the wilderness. In Vancouver's harbor, you can see ships at loading docks. Tugboats haul barges loaded with logs or wood chips.

Vancouver is the third-largest city in Canada. Almost 2 million people live here. Vancouver is made up of people from many different backgrounds. Here you'll find people from China, India, Pakistan, Korea, the Philippines, and Japan.

Stanley Park is one Vancouver attraction we must visit. It is on about 1,000 acres of rainforest. Stanley Park is the largest city park in North America. Inside the park you can hike miles of trails or you can relax in the sun on the sandy beaches. The park also has a zoo where you can see many kinds of animals, including polar bears.

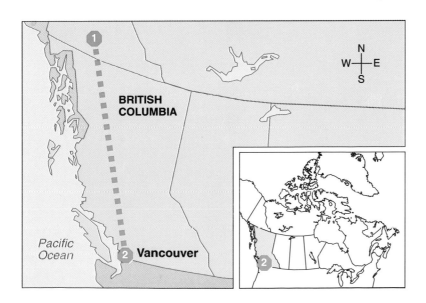

Vancouver's Chinatown

Located in the southeast section of downtown Vancouver is Chinatown. This area contains the second-largest community of Asian people in North America (San Francisco has the largest group). There are hundreds of Chinese restaurants and food stores in Chinatown. Brown ducks and pieces of pork hang in butcher shop windows. *Bok*

Shoppers can find a wide variety of fresh vegetables in Chinatown's bustling, open-air markets.

choy, *gai len*, and *lichee* nuts are heaped on tables in front of open air produce markets. You'll also find shops that sell dried lizards and snakes that are used in making medicine. Many wonderful ornamental gardens can also be found as we wander through this exciting area.

*Now we'll leave Vancouver and sail **east** toward Alberta's beautiful Rocky Mountains.*

Stop 3: Alberta's Rocky Mountains

Bighorn sheep live in Alberta's Rocky Mountains.

The province of Alberta is known for its rugged wilderness. Banff National Park is located in Alberta's Rocky Mountains. It is Canada's oldest park. Besides campers and fishermen, you'll see many moose, bighorn sheep, black bears, mountain goats, grizzlies, and golden eagles.

Jasper National Park is connected to Banff Park by the Icefield Parkway. As you ride on this road, you'll see glaciers, rivers, and waterfalls.

Jasper National Park is located in a wide valley. The Jasper Tramway climbs more than 3,000 feet up a mountain called the Whistlers. From the top of this mountain you can see Mount Robson, which is the highest peak in the Canadian Rockies.

*From here, let's fly **east** to the prairies of Saskatchewan and Manitoba.*

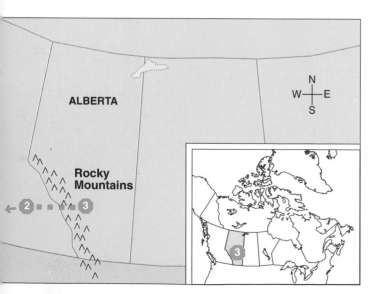

ALBERTA

Rocky Mountains

2 3

Alberta's Rocky Mountains tower over Banff Avenue, which runs through Banff National Park.

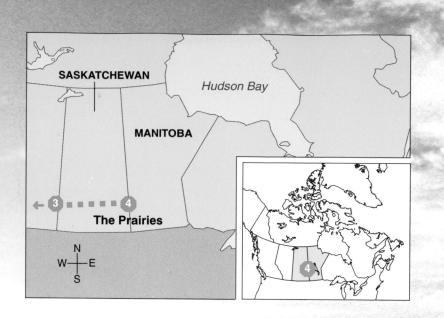

SASKATCHEWAN

Hudson Bay

MANITOBA

3 · · · · · 4

The Prairies

N
W · E
S

Stop 4: The Prairies

Canada's prairies are very different from the Arctic, the seacoast, and the Rocky Mountain areas. As you drop in on the provinces of Saskatchewan and Manitoba, you can't help noticing the rich, dark soil. As far as you can see, the land is covered with wheat. There are other grains growing here, too—barley, rye, and oats—but most of the area produces wheat. Fields cover the prairies like a golden blanket. The land is totally flat and the highways are straight.

The southern areas of the prairie are too dry for growing grain. Ranchers use these grasslands for grazing their cattle. Here, you can see cowboys throwing lariats to rope cattle. Deer and buffalo share the grass with cattle.

Fields of grain stretch for miles along Canada's prairies. Inset: A cowboy ropes a young steer.

*Let's hop into our balloon and ride the winds **southeast** to the busy city of Toronto.*

Hudson Bay

Atlantic
Ocean

ONTARIO

4

N
W   E
S

5

Toronto

5

Stop 5: Toronto

Toronto's harbor area is a wonderful place to visit. There are shops, theaters, and restaurants.

Toronto is Canada's largest city and is in the province of Ontario. It has many special neighborhoods. In the fashion district, you can buy the latest styles of clothing. This district blends into Chinatown on Dundas Street. All the signs in Chinatown are written in English and Chinese.

Toronto also has the world's highest observation deck. It is at the top of the CN (Canadian National) Tower. On a clear day, you can see all the way to Niagara Falls—75 miles away.

Make sure you visit the SkyDome, next to the CN Tower. It is the world's first domed stadium that opens and closes its roof.

The CN Tower is Toronto's tallest structure, high above the city's skyline.

Canada's Wild Animals

Banff National Park is home to many moose and deer.

Canada is home to all kinds of wildlife. Herds of caribou and musk oxen migrate across the tundra. Arctic foxes, hares, wolves, lemmings, and walruses also live in the frigid far north. The polar bear is the king of the Arctic. A polar bear may weigh more than 800 pounds and stand taller than 7 feet on its back legs. It has poor eyesight, but its sense of smell is keen. It can smell a seal a long way off and swim for miles after its prey.

Peaceful bighorn sheep and mountain goats live far above the tree line of the mountains. Farther down among the red cedar and other evergreen trees of the Coast Mountains are black bears, moose, squirrels, rabbits, foxes, and other animals. Mountain lions, mink, and deer inhabit the juniper forests of the Rockies. Buffalo graze in the prairie grasslands.

*Now, let's head **northeast** to Quebec City.*

Polar bears often stand up on their hind legs and look as if they are dancing.

The Chateau
Frontenac Hotel
sits on a hill
above the old
city of Quebec.

Stop 6: Quebec City

Quebec City is in Quebec, Canada's only French-speaking province. The city has winding cobblestone streets and old buildings.

The first thing you notice about Quebec City is that it sits on and around a steep cliff that sticks out into the Saint Lawrence River. The next thing you might see is the wall around the city. Quebec City is the only walled city in Canada. The wall was built more than 200 years ago by the British during the Revolutionary War.

The Chateau Frontenac Hotel is one of the first landmarks you'll see. It is a huge castle. Near the hotel, is the Cathedral of the Holy Trinity.

You can take the steep stairway down the cliff to the Place Royale. This was the first marketplace in Quebec City. It is a great place to find food and buy gifts.

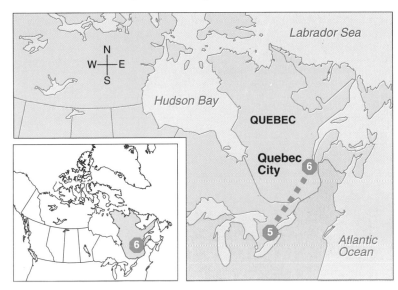

For our final stop in Canada, we'll travel **northeast** to the island of Newfoundland.

Stop 7: The Island of Newfoundland

From the air, the Island of Newfoundland looks like a triangle or an arrowhead pointing out into the Atlantic Ocean. Most of the island is a wilderness of forest, lakes, moors, bogs, and mountains. Most of the people live along the coastline.

The northern peninsula of the island is great for whale watching. It's also a good spot to see icebergs. During the summer months, about 150 icebergs can be spotted. These huge chunks of ice may be 300 feet high.

Throughout the summer, a ferry carries people from another Canadian province, Nova Scotia, to Argentia on the Island of Newfoundland. The air along the coast smells like salt. As

Many fishermen make a living by fishing the waters off the coast of Newfoundland.

Rowboats are used by local people and visitors to travel through Petty Harbour in Newfoundland.

you pass villages, you can see squid hanging on clotheslines to dry. You can also see fishermen unloading their fish or mending nets.

Now it's time to set sail for home. When you return, you can think back on the wonderful adventure you had in Canada.

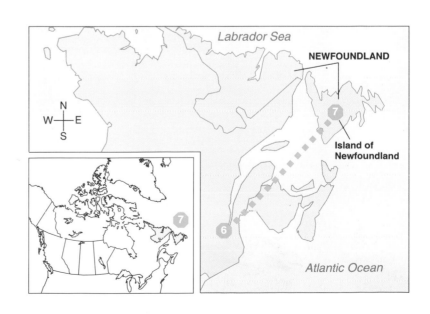

The Language of Newfoundlanders

Some Newfoundlanders think of themselves as being separate from other Canadians—perhaps separate from all other people.

Newfoundlanders even have some of their own special words. Here are a few of these words and what they mean. Try putting some of the words together to make sentences.

Newfoundland Words	English Meaning
Angishore	weak, miserable person
Crubeens	pickled pig's feet
Duckish	time between sunset and dark
Gansey	woolen sweater
Gilderoy	proud person
Jinker	bad-luck person
Oonshick	stupid person
Shooneen	move backwards
Suent	graceful
Squabby	jelly-soft
Silver thaw	sleet or frozen rain
Lolly	soft ice in the harbor
Yaffle	armful of fried fish

Further Reading

Bailey, Donna. *Canada*. Madison, NJ: Raintree Steck-Vaughn, 1992.

Haskins, Jim. *Count Your Way Through Canada*. Minneapolis, MN: Carolrhoda Books, 1989.

Kalman, Bobbie and Schaub, Janine. *Canada—The Land*. Ossining: NY: Crabtree, 1993.

_____. *Canada—The People*. Ossining: NY: Crabtree, 1993.

LeVert, Suzanne. *Let's Discover Canada*. New York: Chelsea House, 1991.

_____. *Nova Scotia*. New York: Chelsea House, 1991.

Murphy, Jack and Murphy, Wendy. *Toronto*. Woodbridge, CT: Blackbirch Press, 1992.

Williams, A. Susan. *Canada*. New York: Franklin Watts, 1991.

Index

Acknowledgments and Photo Credits
Cover: ©Lawrence Migdale/Photo Researchers, Inc.; pp. 4, 6: National Aeronautics and Space Administration; pp. 10, 12: Yukon Government Photo; pp. 14, 16: The Province of British Columbia; pp. 18, 19, 24 (bottom): Alberta Tourism; pp. 20, 21, 24 (top): Saskatchewan Tourism; pp. 22, 28, 29: ©Industry, Science and Technology Canada Photo; p. 25: ©Dan Guravich/Photo Researchers, Inc.; p. 26: ©Porterfield/Chickering/Photo Researchers, Inc. Maps by Blackbirch Graphics, Inc.